An Advent of Understanding

Facing the First Christmas
After the Death of a Loved One

GW00645070

Resurrection Press
An Imprint of
CATHOLIC BOOK PUBLISHING CORP.
Totowa • New Jersey

First published in September, 2007 by Resurrection Press, Catholic Book Publishing Corporation.

Copyright © 2007 by Mary Gay Moore

ISBN 978-1-933-066-07-3

Library of Congress Catalog Number: 2007928276

Quotations from the nonbiblical texts of the *Liturgy of the Hours* © 1974 by International Committee on English in the Liturgy, Inc., Washington, DC. Reproduced with permission. All rights reserved

Scripture quotations from the Old Testament are from the *New Revised Standard Version Bible:* Catholic Edition, copyright © 1993 and 1989 by the National Council of the Churches of Christ in the U.S.A. Used by permission. All rights reserved.

Psalm quotations are from *The Psalms, New Catholic Version of the Bible,* copyright © 2002 by Catholic Book Publishing Corp. Used by permission. All rights reserved.

Cover design by Beth DeNapoli

Cover photo by Michael David Moore

Printed in the U.S.A.

1 2 3 4 5 6 7 8 9

An
Advent
of
Understanding

DEDICATION
To John—
I love you, Colonel.
It was worth every minute.

—·—·—·—

Acknowledgments

These meditations are for those who have encouraged me during my time of searching, especially my beloved late husband John, who supports me from his eternal reward; our children, Michael and Kathleen; the priests whose spiritual guidance continues to be a beacon in my darkness; and other widows: Our Blessed Mother Mary, my own late mother, and my widowed friends, whose courage and perseverance have been an inspiration and an example. Special thanks go to Emilie Cerar, my editor at Resurrection Press, whose kindness and patience were heartwarming and whose every suggestion was an improvement, not a correction.

Contents

First Week of Advent

Darkness

THE FIRST SUNDAY OF ADVENT

Know that the Lord is coming and with him all His saints; that day will dawn with a wonderful light.

**Evening Prayer I, *Liturgy of the Hours,*
First Sunday of Advent**

THANKSGIVING WAS ONLY THREE DAYS AGO and there has already been the predictable media coverage of the annual shopping frenzy and the beginning of the Christmas season.

It is a beginning in the strictest sense of the word for me, and my heart fills with dread and anguish as I look toward the coming month of greatest joy with the deepest of sadness, remembering my husband John's death a few months ago.

One morning he left the house for his weekly tennis game, only to collapse and die within thirty minutes following an hour's play. I remember viewing the remainder of that day, and my life ever since, as through shattered glass. To put it simply, nothing for me will ever be the same again. How I have lived through the intervening months is a mystery and a miracle. I suppose it is simply a matter of putting one foot in front of the other and relying on my own resources, the encouragement of friends, and the strength of God. In retrospect I have no idea how I managed. Now in the days of waning light and falling temperatures, I am challenged both by faith and custom to deck the halls and to be jolly.

I am reminded, in the Evening Prayer antiphon from today's *Liturgy of the Hours*, of Gabriel's admonition to Mary not to be afraid. But her unease was of a different sort, and involved the stirrings of hope and awe, rather than despair and emptiness. She was looking forward, and I am looking back. All of Advent teaches us to look ahead, and, if possible, to overlook the shallow, secular enticements of food, gifts and parties and instead to anticipate with wonder and humility the birth of the tiny child in Bethlehem. Yet my looking back is almost instinctive, as I remember nearly forty Christmases as a wife and face my first one as a widow. The backwash of emptiness and longing and the feeling of being totally overwhelmed are almost more than I can bear.

My hope is to find some kind of guidance, as the Magi did, to illuminate my path and to help me to realize that the great joy and peace of Christmas transcends our human condition. Whether it is our spouse, child, parent, sibling, or dear friend who has died, we are being drawn into the light of the eternal God, even as we continue our struggle toward him on earth in our darkness and sorrow.

Lead, Kindly Light, amidst the tumult and gloom,
Lead Thou me on;
The night is dark, and I am far from home,
Lead Thou me on. **Cardinal John Henry Newman**

THE FIRST MONDAY OF ADVENT

God darkens the mind only in order to give a more perfect light.   **Thomas Merton**

THE SYMBOLISM OF LIGHT at Christmas is, ironically, almost obliterated by the blinding brilliance of artificial illumination. The national Christmas tree in Washington, D.C., and New York's giant tree in Rockefeller Center are festooned not with delicate white tapers or stars but by giant electric balls of various colors. Subdivision homes compete with one another for the best decorative lighting, featuring everything from Frosty and Rudolph to the American flag and an occasional Nativity scene. Floodlit reindeer graze near spiral trees and flashing strands of rainbow bulbs on rooftop gutters. When I was little we used to drive through our neighborhoods to look at the displays. Invariably, my father would comment that a particularly garish house reminded him of a bar and grill. Today I shudder at the blinding glare that surrounds me and I feel disoriented and afraid, like a deer frozen by the headlights of an oncoming car.

The loss of a loved one does this to us. The absence of the person who was the light of our life plunges us into darkness, and like the deer in the headlights, we too are immobilized with fear and bewilderment. Which way do we go, where do we turn? Physically and mentally we shut down while life swirls around us, leaving us frozen and isolated. When John first died I moved through the day feeling like I was encased in a bell jar, a character in a movie with no color or sound. The idea of going to a restaurant was appalling. Laughter and superficial chatter seemed grotesque. Grocery shopping for one was so painful: milk by the quart, 2 apples. I was no longer buying food to prepare dinners for two; it was simply survival. People shopping for their own groceries appeared not to notice me, which was puzzling. I felt as though I was bleeding, that my wounds must show. Why weren't people looking at me with curiosity and compassion? Couldn't they tell that I could barely stand? In many ways this is still true. There is that awful sense of groping in the dark, grasping for stability.

This light that we seek, especially in the days and weeks before Christmas, does not come from neon Santas or blazing Yule logs. *"The true light that enlightens everyone was coming into the world"* (Jn 1:9), writes St. John the Evangelist. And yes, the commercialism of Christmas can disorient us, as can profound sorrow. How, then, can we see more clearly?

Sometimes we simply need to close our eyes. This does not make things darker, it makes things calmer. We have all had the experience of leaving a crowded gathering or a noisy restaurant and welcoming the quiet darkness outside. This is what our Advent searching must be, not stumbling toward the dazzle of frivolity but looking for *"the light of the human race; the light that shines in the darkness"* (Jn 1:4-5).

Even though I wander through the valley of the shadow of death, I fear no evil, for you are at my side.　　**Ps 23:4**

FIRST TUESDAY OF ADVENT

They meet with darkness in the daytime, and grope at noonday as in the night. **Job 5:14**

THE PAIN OF GRIEF following the loss of a loved one makes the brightness of the Christmas season seem like a painful paradox. Simply moving through the day is difficult enough without having to endure the festivities of others that we have no desire to join. How do we face punch and cookies, gift exchanges, dinner parties or even carolers who assure us that *"a turkey and some mistletoe help to make the season bright"*[1] when our hearts are broken? For the first time in many years, our beloved will not be under that mistletoe and the brightness doesn't shine for us.

I just want to sleep through the entire month of December. Or do I really? What else is fear but a rejection of the trust we must have that God, in all things, knows what is best for us? If I say I want to avoid Christmas, am I not saying that Christ's birth, his transformation of mankind from condemnation to redemption, is less important than my own sorrow? This is not only selfish and petulant, it is also an affront to God, whose only son is the very reason for the celebration.

What is it that I'm so afraid of ? Young children can sometimes be afraid of the dark because they can't see "what's out there." For adults, it's not the visual part

---

[1] *The Christmas Song*, Mel Tormé, 1946

that frightens us, it's the fear of the unknown. No one can understand what being a widow or widower is like until it happens to them. I always knew that the death of a spouse left the other person alone; what I didn't understand was that when we lose a spouse, we lose half of ourselves too. I know that I am not the person I was before John's death. Over thirty-nine years, we had so blended our minds and personalities as to truly become "one flesh." Separating the two does irreparable damage, like trying to remove a stamp from an envelope.

When John died, he took part of me with him forever. All at once I had to change completely. I had to learn how to do things that I had never done before. No one would take care of me as he had, and suddenly I was totally responsible for everything in my own life and all I owned. Like many women in my era, I went directly from being my parents' child to my husband's wife. The security was wonderful, but self reliance and independence were somewhat set aside. Now as a middle-aged adult I have had to learn not only how to pay bills and set mousetraps, but also who I am . . . and it is frightening.

In her book *The Year of Magical Thinking,* author Joan Didion tells of her own husband's sudden death. She writes, *"For forty years I saw myself through his eyes. I did not age. This year for the first time since I was in my twenties, I saw*

[2] Joan Didion, *The Year of Magical Thinking* (New York: Alfred A. Knopf, 2005), 197.

myself through the eyes of others. I realized that my image of myself was of someone significantly younger. We are imperfect mortal beings, aware of that mortality even as we push it away, so wired that when we mourn our losses we also mourn, for better or for worse, ourselves. As we were. As we are no longer."[2]

John died a few months ago. In some ways it seems like a long time, but for the most part it seems like only a few hours. When a loved one dies, time freezes that moment in the mind forever, making it always present. I am astonished that I have lived this long not only alone without him, but also still sane and able to function. My life was torn in two and the pieces handed back to me. I don't know fully who I am, now that I am without him. But I know that God knows, and for right now that is all I need. He will somehow help me through this dark night.

And there will be no more night. They will have no need for light from a lamp or from the sun, for the Lord God will give them light, and they will reign forever and ever.

Rev 22:5

FIRST WEDNESDAY OF ADVENT

Praise be to you, Lord, for the feast of your word prepared for us by the apostles, giving us light and joy.

Morning Prayer, *Liturgy of the Hours,*
Feast of St. Andrew

I AM FEELING OVERWHELMED after a flurry of pre-holiday events that made the past week unusually full and active. Two rare dinners out, a class to teach and dinner at the home of friends kept me busy and cheerful and feeling normal, but suddenly the last voice has died away and the house and my heart are once more still and empty. Perhaps I thought foolishly that I was returning to some sort of normalcy after so many long months, but once again I am filled with the anxiety, nausea, and near-panic that I have suffered for so long. I feel off balance and flattened once again.

Especially at Christmastime, it is difficult to socialize without a spouse. Friends say it doesn't matter, but it does matter to the one who arrives and leaves alone. Some things do well on their own—hats, scarves—but one glove or one sock is useless and somehow pathetic without a mate. We see them periodically, lying on a fence or at the curb as if hoping to find their matching partner, but it seldom happens. Things that come in pairs are forlorn when one is lost.

At Mass this morning, as always, I felt overwhelmed. Even the hackneyed hymn "On Eagles' Wings" caused tears to run as I knelt there, surrounded by couples and families. I am often moved during the Consecration and Communion, as I give myself to the only One who really consoles me, sustains me, and possesses me. At the same time I am bereft in my own right as I realize that John's space next to me in the pew is vacant. After receiving the Eucharist I feel as though I somehow have a "direct line" to heaven and can communicate with John in a manner that I can't at other times. I think this is because he now rests eternally in God, the same God whom I have just received, and somehow we are all together in a special way.

The first Christmas must have been like that for those who knelt before the manger, because all at once they were in the physical presence of the One for whom they had been searching, and the long dark nights of wandering on unfamiliar roads were over.

In another pew I notice a couple who are grieving the loss of their daughter who left behind a young boy—their first grandchild. Together, and certainly with others in the church, we seek the comfort and strength of the Eucharist without whom our lives are so raw and empty that we can barely breathe.

Dear Jesus, let me find you as I walk hesitantly in this darkness. I feel so lost and abandoned. Lead me into your light as you did the shepherds, Magi, and all who found you in Bethlehem. Let me remember that your light is never extinguished and will always be a beacon if we only keep searching for it.

For all of you are children of the light and children of the day. We do not belong to the night or to the darkness.

1 Thes 5:5

FIRST THURSDAY OF ADVENT

From the darkness comes light. From death, life. From the abyss there comes, unaccountably, the mysterious gift of the Spirit sent by God to make all things new, to transform the created and redeemed world, and to re-establish all things in Christ.

Thomas Merton, *Contemplative Prayer*

THE CALENDAR PAGE TURNS to December and the Christmas season is now here in earnest. People seem to enjoy the self-imposed frenzy and rush. It's almost as if they don't want to slow down to see what Advent is for. Advent is like turning off the main highway and onto a country road at night. There are no street signs, no highway billboards. The stars and perhaps the moon light up the darkness with calm and brilliance. It is beautiful, but the road is unmarked. How do we find our way on an unmarked road, especially in the dark? Isn't that the question of Advent, the question of grief, the question of faith? How did we get onto this road and how do we get back to the main one? Do we even want to?

It was like that for many centuries before the birth of Christ. People were wandering and rootless, with little faith that God would provide for them. Losing hope in the promised Messiah, God's Chosen People were suffering the same harshness of life as everyone else. Wars, illness and death, famines, floods and poverty were their lot and they were discouraged and skeptical despite the reassurance of the prophets.

Grief is like that, too. About three weeks after John died, another widow at church assured me, *"I promise it will get better. Eventually you'll feel fine again."* Like the Israelites, I am tired of waiting and doubtful of a respite, yet I find myself ashamed to feel this way. The promise of a Messiah, the promise of a brighter day ahead, the guarantee of our redemption through Christ's birth, life, death, and resurrection are all sacred covenants from God. With John by my side I could be happy and grateful; without him I am filled with doubt.

During Advent, we seek to escape the glare of the world and observe the quiet starlight, especially from that one special star that led the Magi to Bethlehem. When one is grieving and missing a loved one, that sort of soothing darkness can be a welcome change.

There is a method of natural childbirth, developed by the French obstetrician Dr. Frederick Leboyer, in which a baby is born in a room with very little light. The darkness is soothing and helps to soften the baby's abrupt entry into the world, normally lit by the glaring lights of most delivery rooms. The vulnerable and traumatized infant cannot face bright lights yet, and needs time to adjust to its new surroundings. So it is with sorrow. When one is in grief and missing a loved one, too much light is harsh and painful. We need time to adjust to our new surroundings of loss and pain.

I will look for the gradual dawn of the light of my recovery in the darkness of Advent, which heralds the birth of the Light of the World.

O Dawn of the East, brightness of the light eternal, and Sun of Justice: Come, and enlighten them that sit in darkness and in the shadow of death.

Liturgy of the Hours, **Vespers, December first**

FIRST FRIDAY OF ADVENT

The seed is in darkness: the darkness of sorrow, the darkness of faith.   **Caryll Houselander**

ON THIS FIRST ADVENT FRIDAY, those who pray the *Liturgy of the Hours* rejoice with Jerusalem that her light will come, that the Lord will dawn on her in radiant beauty. This promise of hope and salvation is renewed daily in nature with every new dawn. Light and optimism go together, as do despair and darkness. Scientific studies have shown higher instances of depression during winter months when there are fewer hours of daylight, in a phenomenon known as Seasonal Affective Disorder. Sacred Scripture—especially St. John's Gospel—is filled with imagery connecting light and God, and in the Creed we profess Jesus as "Light from Light." St. Justin Martyr describes beautifully how Christ's light, begotten of the Father's, is like lighting one flame from another without the new one diminishing its source. During Advent we light a special wreath, adding a new candle each week. Gradually the darkness fades and the light increases as we anticipate the coming of Jesus, the Light of the World. Light symbolizes life. Without light, we cannot see. Without light, we cannot grow. Without light, we cannot live. Without the light of God in our souls and hearts, we can neither love him nor love others in him.

When we love someone so much that that person becomes a part of us, we are plunged into a kind of darkness at their death. Their absence takes some of the light from our life and we are unable to see our way out of the gloom of despair and heartache. That is why the first Christmas without them is both painful and therapeutic, because now more than ever before we need the light of Christ to illuminate our path and clarify our vision. We need the promise of God's Son to bring brightness to our soul, if not to our emotions. In *The Imitation of Christ*, Thomas à Kempis wrote: *"You have given Your holy Body to strengthen my weak mind and body, and You have given your Word for a lamp to my feet. Without these two things I cannot live as I ought, for the Word of God is the light of my soul, and Your Sacrament the Bread that gives me life."*

Anyone who has ever flown eastward on an overnight flight can remember seeing the first rays of daybreak on the horizon. After hours of total darkness, we can observe the faintest suggestion of a soft, greenish light at the edge of the horizon. The effect is stunning. It is more than a diurnal routine; it feels like a miracle. Gradually the light brightens and the colors of dawn deepen to hues reminiscent of beach glass—green and blue, then peach and rose. And it is more than light, it is a promise of the oncoming day, the nearing destination, and the start of an adventure or opportunity, even if it is just a routine trip.

Following a death, the last thing we want is to step back into brightness, to face the dazzle of lights. And yet this is what we must do. The timetable is ours. The grieving process does not necessarily take one year, as some say. It can take a lifetime . . . or less. But our nature struggles to regain equilibrium, like a newborn foal attempting to stand. We want to get better; we want to live; we want to face the rest of our lives with curiosity and gratitude and, if possible, with joy. And so we turn toward the light.

We are born in Christ today. . . . Can it be surprising that we feel in our hearts the exultation of the divine light which streams into our spirit from the presence of the newborn Savior, and transforms us from glory to glory in his image? This is the mystery of light which shines on us today.

Thomas Merton

FIRST SATURDAY OF ADVENT

Your light will come, Jerusalem; the Lord will dawn on you in radiant beauty.

Morning Prayer, *Liturgy of the Hours,*
First Saturday of Advent

SATURDAY, OUR LADY'S DAY. Mary was one of the main participants in the Advent-Christmas story. In fact, her story is all the more amazing because she was a human being like us, and the most extraordinary thing in all of history that could have happened to a human being happened to her. She was a young, naïve, pious Jewish girl from Galilee, yet she became the Mother of God.

One seldom-mentioned aspect of Mary's life is that she was a widow. Had St. Joseph been alive at the time of Our Lord's death, he would have been at the foot of the Cross with Mary and John, the Beloved Disciple. His name would certainly have been mentioned in the Gospel, but it was not. That means that not only was Mary without her beloved spouse, but also that she had to endure the unspeakable anguish of watching, alone, as her son was nailed to a cross and died. One can meditate on the Pietà and realize how much easier it would have been had Joseph been there to help Mary cradle the body of Christ in his strong arms. Her sense of isolation must have nearly overwhelmed her as she gazed at the gray, bloodstained face of the Savior and realized that he was her flesh and blood, remembering a happier time when she had looked down on him in the manger in Bethlehem the night he was born. No darkness of soul in history ever compared to this, yet she survived.

Perhaps we are quick to say, "Oh, but she was special because God had always planned for her to be the mother of the savior." This is true, but we are special in God's eyes as well, and he knows that we can meet the challenges he sends us and rise to them with his help. No one ever "promised us a rose garden," and almost no one is spared the sorrow of losing a family member. Mary did not have any extra defenses to protect her from the sorrow of Christ's death. What she did have were the two essential things: trust and love of God. When she said "Let it be done to me according to your word," (Lk 1:38) she didn't add "except for the difficult parts."

Perhaps it is a lesson for those of us who mourn, that if the God-bearer could withstand, without the support of her husband, the brutal death of her son, then we too can face the rest of our life's challenges with the help of God and our loved ones. In the depths of her anguish, Mary was nonetheless secure in knowing that God and St. Joseph were with her and supporting her from heaven. Despite our fears, anxieties and loneliness, God can work miracles in us if we can somehow, like Mary, murmur a weak but sincere "fiat" to his will.

✳

*Father in heaven, the day draws near when the glory of
your Son will make radiant the night of the waiting
world.*

Evening Prayer I, *Liturgy of the Hours,*
Second Sunday of Advent

Second Week of Advent

Stillness

SECOND SUNDAY OF ADVENT

In the snow, under the fall of snow, the world becomes an Advent place, waiting quietly, waiting for whatever destiny the snow may bring.

Mitch Finley, *Season of Promises*

I REMEMBER AS A CHILD the wonderful silence outdoors after a blizzard. Sounds were muffled as if the world was wrapped in cotton. That lovely frozen fluff on the ground absorbed the normally harsh noises of daily life, and everything sounded as though it was through a closed door. The stillness was beautiful. Everything seemed slower and calmer.

Silence can be upsetting, too. There is nothing so still as even a small home where a loved one lived and now has died. Those who are left alone feel imprisoned and invisible. With no other human life to share, with no sounds of running water, turning pages, footsteps, or voices, we can quickly feel tremendously isolated. Even now I listen for the most common noises—a laugh, a beer-can tab being pulled, the rustle of the newspaper. There is not a single sound and I feel entombed.

The saintly Mahatma Gandhi wrote: *"In the attitude of silence the soul finds the path in a clearer light, and what is elusive and deceptive resolves itself into crystal clearness."* It's true that silence not only allows one to think, but also to digest those thoughts, make plans, and evaluate one's circumstances. It seems that since John's death, I can think of nothing else. The silence makes his absence more pronounced, perhaps because I am unconsciously listening for indications that he is there. The emptiness is engulfing and my modest house seems as large as a castle. But although I feel isolated, I also feel, sometimes more keenly than others, that somehow he is with me, and that free from his earthly bonds he views me from eternity and knows what is going on inside my head. And, conversely, I can talk to him and share my thoughts and even ask his guidance and advice. It's a fact that John is no longer here. But he is with God, and God is here; therefore, in a way which we cannot understand, John is also here. I talk to him, often aloud, without guilt or embarrassment.

Is this prayer? Certainly. Has this ever been done before? Countless times, both between those who have died and those left behind, and also between those who are yet to be born and those waiting for them. Our Lady spent nine months in meditation and prayer to the Infant growing in her womb, sharing in silence her thoughts of wonder, awe, humility, and perhaps more than a little uncertainty.

"Nothing in all creation is so like God as stillness," wrote Meister Eckhart, the great fourteenth century mystic. But this stillness mustn't simply be a vacuum, an absence of noise. It has to be an expectant, productive silence which is full of the sound of God. And what is the sound of God? I liken it to the high frequency sound made by whistles that human ears can't hear, only canine ears. I think the sound of God is similar, because it doesn't resonate like ordinary conversation. Rather, it is the "tiny whispering sound" heard by the prophet Elijah (1 Kings 19:12) which is never more meaningful than during Advent, when the whole world seems to turn up its volume of noisy shoppers, carolers, and party-goers. The media screams about sales and bargains, parties and parades, lights and bands and revelry. Yet the Christ child was born in a remote barn, without any crowds, lulled to sleep by the soft, rhythmic sound of the animals' breathing.

We will never be in tune with the sound of God during Advent if we make so much noise that we can't hear Him. Advent means "coming," and if we don't want to miss his coming, we have to be quiet and listen.

Silence is the strength of our interior life. . . . If we fill our lives with silence, then we will live in hope.

Thomas Merton

SECOND MONDAY OF ADVENT

The world in solemn stillness lay to hear the angels sing.
  Christmas carol, " It Came Upon a Midnight Clear"

WHEN ONE IS IN MOURNING, noises can be grating on the ears and on the psyche, laughter in particular. The first Christmas alone is excruciating, no matter what others do to try to ease the pain. It is so difficult to face the most joyful day in the year without the person who shared two-thirds of my life. How can other people be so cheerful? Who cares about 50% off sales, party menus, lighting ideas, and gift wrap? Christmas songs on the radio and in the grocery store are painful: "Merry Christmas, Darling," "I'll Have a Blue Christmas Without You," "I'll Be Home for Christmas, but Only in My Dreams" are all guarantees of hasty exits and welling tears. Yet shoppers and pageant participants carry on blissfully unaware of the pain of one of the loneliest groups on earth, the recently bereaved. How can I face this, how can I bear it, remembering all our happy Christmases together?

Time marches on. We can't stop the dawn from breaking, the buds from bursting, the leaves from falling. Things move inexorably toward their maturation and eventually their death. The Book of Ecclesiastes puts it this way: *To everything there is a season and a time for every purpose under heaven. A time to be born and a time to die. . . . A time to weep and a time to laugh; a time to mourn and a time to dance"* (Eccl 3:1-4). So while we who grieve leak tears and grip the pew during Mass to keep from keening, the noise of the merrymakers will someday be silenced by grief as well. It is a universal experience. It makes life itself an echo, and is like being sealed into a cave. For now we must summon our resources and try to hear God's voice somewhere in the stillness.

What is the answer to our profound sorrow and loneliness? First of all, we must face the silence for what it is. In that silence we can remember the sounds of our loved one's voice, our discussions, our laughter, our children. We can remember sounds we shared together: pounding surf, phone calls, shouting in the snow, whispers in the night, shared promises, mealtime conversation, reminiscences. Then, we can listen to a silence rich with memories.

Life goes on. A bird calls, the wind blows, a plane flies overhead. God lets life go on. The phone rings, the coffee perks, the mail truck comes down the street. God lets life go on. And in the depths of our aching hearts, we can listen for the voice of God himself, who promises to be with us in our grief, to keep his yoke easy and his burden light. He will remind us of his beloved son in the silent Garden of Gethsemane, who for a few moments in the depths of his anguished humanity, doubted his ability to go on, and cried out to be relieved of such tremendous suffering.

He was a man of sorrows, and acquainted with grief. He was silent and opened not His mouth. **Isa 53:3, 7**

SECOND TUESDAY OF ADVENT

Let us continue to be still for a while longer, to become yet a little more full of the God who dwells within.

Caryll Houselander

THIS, THEN, IS AN IMPORTANT TOOL with which to dig oneself out of grief, especially in this season of others' visible joy and celebration. It is the need to turn the silence of emptiness and the darkness of confusion into ways of regrouping, healing and planning.

Darkness and silence can be lonely, but they are also necessary for rest. We cannot sleep with our eyes wide open in the sunlight, or think clearly amid the din of heavy traffic in Times Square. To restore ourselves we must have both darkness and silence. But instead of the bleak darkness of our outlook after losing our loved ones, and the lonely echo in our home when their voice is silenced, we need to learn how to turn, as Mary did, to the Son of God whom she nurtured in the silence and life-giving darkness of her womb during Advent. It was a period of quiet growth and development, not of stagnation.

With widowhood comes a terrible feeling of being paralyzed, of not wanting to join in others' festivities, of not wanting to celebrate, even the birth of Jesus Christ. Too many Christmas traditions are tied to memories of our loved ones, so it is normal that they are painful. It is not necessary, however, either to recapture Christmases that will never come again or to do nothing in order to avoid the pain. My first Christmas as a widow, our pastor gently urged me to get a tree, and I did so reluctantly. Looking at all the family ornaments made me so sad that I couldn't hang them. So I compromised and hung only angels and John's special ornaments, and it was lovely. It was a step, even though a small one, and I knew that John would want me to continue, to grow, to experience life in all its fullness.

At the Annunciation, Mary did not know what lay ahead either for herself or for her son, but she knew that she had to do all she could to aid the development of the child within her, primarily through rest, nutrition, and quiet. Christ is, will be, and must be my nourishment—his body and blood, the food of angels and also the food of the weak, the frightened and the lonely—that will sustain me as the human bodies of Christ and Mary sustained each other, even as he grew within her. And Christ will also be my rest if only I can allow him to be, if only I can stop clenching, shaking, sighing and being afraid and turn to him, as Mary rested in the Lord while he rested in her womb.

When John died, in those first awful hours when people came over to share my shock and disbelief, I had several people offer to stay with me. I thanked them but kept saying no, that I couldn't think straight, that I needed silence. Their voices seemed brittle and cacophonous and I needed to come to grips on my own with what had happened and to think about what to do next. I simply had to have quiet in which to do that. In the *Liturgy of the Hours,* Sunday night Compline reminds us: *"Fear Him; do not sin: ponder on your bed and be still"*(Ps 4:5). We cannot heal, nor make decisions, when there is a racket going on. Nonetheless, sending away the neighbors cannot silence the demons within.

Let us try to include moments of silence in our own lives that we may listen to the will of the Father.

Dom Augustine Moore, OCSO,
Within the Heart of Mary

SECOND WEDNESDAY OF ADVENT

Still, still, still,
One can hear the falling snow.
For all is hushed,
The world is sleeping,
Holy Star its vigil keeping.
Still, still, still,
One can hear the falling snow.

Traditional Austrian carol

NO ONE IS MORE DEVOTED to silence than the monks and nuns of the Trappist order. They offer their gift of non-essential speech to God so that they may better hear his voice in their hearts without any distraction. Other monastic orders, such as the Carthusians, do the same. Perhaps the most well-known Trappist was Fr. Louis, OCSO, whose secular name was Thomas Merton. He wrote extensively about interior silence. The following piece was originally published in *The Baptist Student,* the newspaper of the Southern Baptist Theological Seminary in Louisville, Kentucky (vol. 48, no. 5, February 1969):

Silence has many dimensions. It can be a regression and an escape, a loss of self, or it can be presence, awareness, unification, self-discovery. Negative silence blurs and confuses our identity and we lapse into daydreams or diffuse anxieties. Positive silence pulls us together and makes us realize who we are, who we might be, and the distance between these two.

Hence, positive silence implies a disciplined choice, and what Paul Tillich called the "courage to be." In the long run, the discipline of creative silence demands a certain kind of faith. For when we come face to face with ourselves in the lonely ground of our own being, we confront many questions about the value of our existence, the reality of our commitments, the authenticity of our everyday lives.

Nowhere is this truer than for someone who grieves. There is a strong tendency to pull the covers over our head and "burrow under," to avoid our friends and family and life itself out of a sense of futility and sadness. In addition to losing someone we love, we sometimes run the risk of losing ourselves in the process, because of the feeling that our loved ones have taken half of us with them. This is indeed "negative silence." But Merton points out the need for the positive silence of recognizing our potential in God. It takes strength. It takes courage. And yes, it is a choice, but one which we must make repeatedly if we are to survive and be true to our calling to be all that God expects of us. It is important to remind ourselves that the one we mourn would have expected nothing less. No one who truly loved us would say, "When I die I want you to give up, stop living, and be sad for the rest of your life."

How long will it take to come to this point of realization? It varies for everyone. At least several months, often years. Perhaps a lifetime. But like Sisyphus' rock, it is the daily burden which we must push ahead of us, with the assistance of God's great grace.

In the silence of our hearts, there's a voice that stirs within

We don't know what happens here until we listen.

In the silence of our hearts we keep in touch with our world

We see the ups and downs of our lives as the years pass by.

It is the Lord who speaks to us in the silence of our hearts

He lets us feel His love and gives us life again.

Hymn by Fr. Noel Gomez, La Paz,
Iloilo City, Philippines

SECOND THURSDAY OF ADVENT

Here a woman wrapped in silence, and the words were closed within her spacious heart for pondering.

John Lynch, *A Woman Wrapped in Silence*

SILENCE CAN BE UPSETTING; on the other hand, the sound of crying is harsh. Tears are cathartic but such a breakdown; literally, a loss of control. And it's an assault on the calm of the day. Although I feel better after tears, I also feel spent and empty and very alone. It doesn't bring John back or alleviate the brokenness of my heart. Carrying on is really a way of railing against fate and is commonplace to the majority of humans, with one likely exception: Mary of Nazareth.

I think about her in a special way today, the Feast of the Immaculate Conception. Although we know little about her, it is probable that Our Lady never made loud noises in protest of her fate. At first she must have felt bewildered and uncertain but eventually she accepted everything that happened to her as the will of God. Why was she like that? After all, she was poor and uneducated, a naïve and simple teenager who had not been taught about being tough and courageous in the face of adversity. How could she be so strong? The answer was simple: Mary was "full of grace." Not by genes, not by mental discipline, but because God the Father made her that way from the very instant of her conception. She was, as Caryll

Houselander points out in *The Reed of God*, the very first chalice to hold the precious blood of Christ, and she had to be made spotless, flawless, without mark or blemish of any kind. For nine months her body was a walking tabernacle for the Son of God, and the Holy Spirit could only put the Christ child into a receptacle that was pure and immaculate in all ways. So when things happened to her that she did not understand, which filled her with pain and broke her heart, she was silent. This was due in part to her virtue, but that virtue stemmed from her perfection. She was silent because of her total acceptance of God's will for her, ordained from the beginning of time and enacted from the day on which she was conceived. She gave her assent to the angel and quietly accepted everything that occurred after that. She trusted God and was still—not only in her lack of verbal questioning and complaining but in her demeanor and her gentle humility. She didn't understand, but she put her faith in God and that was enough.

How does Mary's quiet acceptance set an example for those who grieve? Surely we don't understand when our loved ones are taken out of our lives. Mary also lost her parents, her husband and her son, and certainly her grief was as difficult as any woman's would be. But she acquiesced to God's plan. She knew that in his divine providence there were things she couldn't comprehend, but she trusted. And thus she was still and submissive, and offered her grief back to God as a gift. Later she held the broken body of her son in her arms on Calvary and again offered him back to his Father in a spirit of quiet acceptance. She didn't fully understand, nor do we. But she knew that somehow it would be all right. She was the holiest woman, wife, and mother who ever lived. Her soul was conceived without sin and remained that way forever, in perfect beauty, perfect trust, perfect stillness.

It was her task to remain faithful to the divine plan, which she adored and meditated on in the silence of her soul. In fact Luke adds, "His Mother kept all these things in her heart." (Lk 2:18-19)

Pope John Paul II, General Audience, July 4, 1990

SECOND FRIDAY OF ADVENT

How silently, how silently, the wondrous gift is given!
So God imparts to human hearts the blessings of His
heaven.
No ear may hear his coming, but in the world of sin,
Where meek souls will receive Him, still, the dear Christ
enters in.

"O Little Town of Bethlehem," Christmas Carol

THIS THEN IS THE SECRET which is revealed when we hear the silence of Advent: the silence of Christ as he enters the world and enters our hearts. When we are mourning, however, the silence can be a challenge. It is painful to be aware of the silence in our lives caused by the death of our loved one. It is painful, too, to listen to the sound of others' celebrations when we do not feel joy ourselves. But we do not live in a vacuum and we must learn to create a new sort of music in our hearts and souls.

Music?? What kind of music can appeal to a broken heart? Upbeat music is a mockery and wistful music can make us feel worse. Birdsong and rustling leaves are a start. There is also the music of crashing waves, a babbling brook, booming thunder. There's perking coffee, lowing cattle, purring kittens. The sounds of life and normalcy, the gentle sounds of the continuum of God's creation, are all soothing sounds of joy and goodness. The empty silence needs to become full—full at least of promise, full of hope, full of trust in God that he will not forget us nor abandon us in our loss. The psalmist tells us: *"The Lord watches over the stranger and sustains the fatherless and the widow"* (Ps 146:9), and also that *"He heals the brokenhearted and bandages their wounds"* (Ps 147:3). The music of creative, expectant silence is soothing to a grieving person's soul and ears as well. It is there that God speaks to us of healing and restoration, of joy in him if not in our actual situation. There are different kinds of joy and those who are alone must have the courage and the strength and the trust in God to search for them.

So much of Christmas is about silence because Jesus was born in a quiet place, away from the clamor of the city. He comes again into our hearts only when we are quiet enough interiorly to prepare a place for him. Mary was silent as she awaited the Messiah's birth. I will try to allow the soothing of a healing, restorative silence prepare my heart and soul for the coming of the Son of God and for a new beginning to my own life.

It is important in your spiritual life to have a few moments when you do not think about God, but be with Him in silence.

Dom Augustine Moore, OCSO,
Within the Heart of Mary

SECOND SATURDAY OF ADVENT

Night and day, why is it so, that this longing for you follows wherever I go?
In the roaring traffic's boom, in the silence of my lonely room, I think of you, day and night, night and day.
                    "Night and Day," Cole Porter, 1934

THE SOUNDS OF SOME MUSIC, when we are grieving, can nearly break our hearts. All couples have songs that carry special meaning for them. I can get into my car feeling relatively calm and hear a song on the radio that will reduce me to floods of tears in a matter of moments. The pain in my chest can feel like fire. All widowed people have felt this and no one else can begin to understand it until it happens to them. What can we do? Many people would say to stop listening to music that unearths nostalgic memories of a happier time, but sometimes the pain is cathartic and the memory very precious. It is important, in those moments, to remember the happy event and not the sad loss, and to rejoice that we had those magnificent memories together. This is probably the hardest part of loss, to balance the current heartache with remembrances of former joy.

The sounds of daily life can be jarring: traffic, loud music, commercials, incessant chatter, cell phones. We must try each day to keep in mind the sounds of past joys, as well as healthy and positive sounds that we hear today. A friend's voice, a ringing phone, the mailman's truck, the hum of appliances, are all signs that life does, in fact, go on. We can try to turn back time but it doesn't work. Gently, the passage of the days turns us toward the road of our own journey, emptier and more difficult without our loved one but still navigable.

We've all seen a toddler lie down and scream when his mother says it's time to go, but eventually he gets up and runs to catch up to her, knowing that he truly wants to be with her. It is the same with us and God. We try in vain to make time go back to the day when our loved one died, but it won't happen. We simply have to go it alone, step by painful step. It is without a doubt the most exhausting, agonizing labor of our entire life. Some days we make little progress; some days we regress. We can be certain, however, that God will wait until we catch up to him. And on those days when we lack the energy and will, he will pick us up and carry us.

Don't cry because it's over, smile because it happened.
Sarah Ackerman

Third Week of Advent

Gaudete—Joy

✳

THIRD SUNDAY OF ADVENT

Gaudete in Domino semper. (Rejoice in the Lord always.)
Introit, Mass of Gaudete Sunday

SOMETHING HAS CHANGED. The achingly dark and empty days of longing for the Christ child are disappearing. In their place is a feeling of hope. It is hard to notice the shift in the secular world because of the glare and din of shopping and parties. But in the Church's liturgy it is very tangible.

First there is the appearance of a third candle, the rose-colored one, in the Advent wreath. One candle gives very little light. Two candles double it, and a third one makes a pronounced difference. The darkness is fading and it is getting brighter.

Second, the priest wears rose vestments this Sunday. Purple robes are beautiful, but they are formal and somber. Rose gladdens the heart and puts one in mind of flowers and joy.

Joy is a hard commodity to find in the minds and hearts of the bereaved. This is true anytime but especially at Christmas when everyone else seems to have a festiveness that we can't summon. We continue to be aware that half of our former self has been cut away and we feel stripped and vulnerable. The rejoicing of Gaudete, however, is of a different sort. It is a joy of something so enormous and beautiful that all the world is swept off its feet, even those who mourn. It is the joy of our salvation. We can look forward to an ordinary lunch with a friend or a visit from our children, but this is altogether *extraordinary,* because what we anticipate is larger than life, larger than sin, larger than death. It is the coming of the Son of God on Christmas, to become one of us, to bless and lead us, and ultimately to save us. Grief, loss, or sorrow cannot prevail in the face of such pure, godly happiness. And so, as the prayers of the day tell us, we must rejoice.

Perhaps the joy of Gaudete Sunday is similar to the feeling Mary experienced when she felt her child move within her for the first time. All at once she realized that he was really there, living and growing in the dark silence of her womb. She knew that this soon-to-be event was bigger than she was and totally out of her hands. This did not make her uneasy, however, because she was reassured that her life and that of her child were totally in the hands of God himself. He would make it work according to his Word.

So it is with our loss. We can't go back, can't change the horrible fact of their death. And yet it is once again the Christmas season, when the entire Christian world turns to observe the birth of a poor Jewish baby who would save all of mankind. And we who believe that this child was God himself know that his coming will eventually wipe away our tears, that we will be reunited with our loved ones and with Our Lord for all eternity in heaven. There are times when the constriction in my chest, from sadness and loneliness, loosens a little, when I think with swelling anticipation of the Savior's birth. I think that that sensation is an early Christmas gift from the Lord.

Prepare our hearts and remove the sadness that hinders us from feeling the joy which His presence will bestow, for he is Lord forever and ever.

Evening Prayer I, *Liturgy of the Hours,*
Gaudete Sunday

THIRD MONDAY OF ADVENT

Thanks be to God for His indescribable gift!

2 Cor 9:15

IN THE TEMPORAL SENSE, Christmas means presents. Whether we are in the Christmas spirit or not, there are people with whom we exchange gifts each year, sometimes because we feel we should, and other times because we really want to. Spiritually, too, we are mindful of all that we have received from Almighty God, and we wonder what we can offer to him in return.

For the first Christmas following the death of our loved one, there is little impetus to either give or receive. We feel as though all we had of value has been taken from us, and it is the only thing we want back. We know that flowers, candy, books, jewelry, or clothing will lie like dust under our tree and mean nothing to us. Nevertheless, two things can make a difference. We need to remember all that God has given us, even though we have lost our great love. It takes real effort to avoid the tendency to be petulant, and to avoid "if only" thoughts. Instead we must focus on the years we did have together, the joy, the memories, the fun, the love. Whether six years or sixty years, it was a blessed time, sweetened by God's many graces and preserved forever in our hearts and dreams.

The other thing that can make a difference is to turn our attention to what we can give to Our Lord at

Christmas. This also takes both effort and imagination. We can give him our heart, it is true, but it feels so broken these days that if he were to touch it, it would probably shatter. Perhaps it would be better to give him what is inside our heart: gratitude, love, and the desire to go on, even with our diminished family, and therefore more in need than ever of his guidance. We can meditate at length on the infant Jesus in the manger on that first Christmas, and how we could have made his bed more comfortable. I imagine this: first, I would line it with pine boughs, the short-needled, soft kind, like cedar, with their wonderful piney fragrance and with all the twigs and cones removed. Then I would add clouds, big, billowy soft ones and I would cover them with Irish linen, with a high thread count, soft and rich and elegant. Next I would put in a piece of the finest silk, fit for a king. It would be the exact color of the sky. Finally, to warm him I would put my heart in the manger next to him, even though I fear it has too many thorns and burrs in it, like a sweetgum ball, which might hurt him and make him cry. I will spend the rest of Advent trying to remove the burrs from my heart for him.

Then they opened their treasure chests and offered him gifts of gold, frankincense, and myrrh.

Mt 2:11

THIRD TUESDAY OF ADVENT

"Why lies He in such mean estate where ox and ass are feeding?"

"What Child is This?" 16th century carol

To me, one of the most beautiful of all Christmas passages is from a very old, anonymous Latin text that describes the Nativity of Our Lord:

> *O magnum mysterium et admirabile sacramentum, ut animalia viderent*
> *Dominum natum jacentem in præsepio.*

The translation is as follows:

> *O great mystery and wondrous sacrament, that animals should see the newborn Lord lying in the manger.*

This concept may be less meaningful for people who are not animal lovers. The very idea of any baby, much less the Son of God, placed in a feed trough requires an attitude adjustment to say the least. Some people think that animals are dirty and likely to carry germs and disease, and for them to have been the first witnesses and worshipers at Christ's birth is hard to fathom. If they could rewrite the story, our Lord would lie, wrapped in costly covers in a spotless crib—protected from the cold night air—a safe distance from any barnyard. But animals, unlike man, are true to the nature which God gave them at creation. No horse has ever sinned, no bird has ever lied, no buffalo has ever betrayed a trust. Animals do not have intellect and free will and therefore cannot choose to go against God's commands. They are simple and live out their lives according to their Creator's design.

The irony of their presence at the Lord's birth is delightful. The beasts' sweet, grassy breath scented the stable and their flanks gave off heat to warm the little Lord's body. Instead of thinking, "What's wrong with this picture?" we should smile with awe and gratitude at the wondrous ways of God, and at the fact that very little about the birth of the Messiah was the way we would have done it! Who else was really pure enough to witness the arrival of Jesus other than these placid beasts? Some may have thought that Mary and Joseph should have made advance lodging arrangements and had a strong, experienced midwife in attendance. Instead, they were alone with their own donkey, some cattle and sheep, and God.

This is the plight of the widow, too, who in the final analysis is without any support outside of her memories and her Lord. Friends and family are wonderful, but they have their own lives to lead. Sometimes the gentle gaze of a pet's eyes can bring more consolation than the well-intentioned but vapid words of other people. But it is God's presence that will ultimately transform all of those who wait in hope, as it did that night in Bethlehem. We look into our own hearts as into the manger and tell God that we are so beaten down by our grief, so humbled before him in our need, that this sorrow is all we have to offer him at his birth. We ask for little in return beyond his presence and his guidance. For us it is enough. He is all we need and in fact, all we have now.

This is the ultimate Christmas gift exchange. We bring him our broken hearts, our longing to stand up again, our fear, our fatigue. And like the donkey and ox, we look into his face and receive back from the Son of God the promise, not only of our loved one's eternal life, but of our own someday as well. Christmas isn't about price rollbacks at Wal-Mart or gold gauze ribbons or Santa or champagne or perfume. It is, however, about gifts and giving, the gift from God of his son to redeem mankind and our gift of welcoming him into our heart.

By the power of your birth, comfort those who are saved.
Evening Prayer I, *Liturgy of the Hours,*
Solemnity of Christmas

THIRD WEDNESDAY OF ADVENT

He will bring to light what is hidden in darkness and will disclose the motives of all hearts.   **1 Cor 4:5**

GIFTS AND JOY. I understand about them. I know that it is the Christmas season. But I am so sad and lonely! What do I do? How do I somehow correlate the ache in my heart at John's death with the love in my heart at Christ's birth? And how can I overlook the fact that I can't give my husband a gift ever again?

What does it mean that "life is changed, not taken away?" We need to remind ourselves that our loved one has not ceased to exist, but has simply stopped living on Earth. If the saints can answer intercessory prayers, they must be able to hear our requests. Who is more likely to listen to us than the one we miss so terribly at this time? I believe with all my heart that we can continue to exchange the gift of love even with those who are no longer physically present.

An hour after John died I felt compelled to put his wedding ring on a chain around my neck and have worn it there ever since. At Mass, I slip it over my finger after receiving Holy Communion. It is a means of connecting myself to John during the most sacred moments on Earth—following the reception of Christ into my own body and soul. If John has joined God in heaven and God joins me on Earth when I receive him, then the three of us are together in a spiritual trio of incredible strength, love, and union. For that short time, bodies don't matter, only God's presence in both of us at the same time and ours in him. It is a joining that transcends the flesh.

The spirit of gift-giving which is Christmas is nowhere more profoundly fulfilled than in the Holy Eucharist. God the Creator gave us the universe and life itself. God the Holy Spirit is the great Activator who guides us on our way and illumines the path, who turns the love of God in our souls into a stimulus that produces both prayer and action in response. But it is the gift of the Son that literally transforms our sinful human flesh into partakers of his own flesh. When he gives us his body at Mass we are united with him, with the other persons of the Trinity, and with all of the souls of the blessed who have gone before us and reached their eternal destiny. The saints in heaven and all our loved ones join us in the Eucharist and seem so close to us in their purified state. They may be far away from us in time and distance but they are intimately present in grace and joy. And we are all united in Christ and in his Body which we have just received. So this gift of myself to John in Christ, which somehow illuminates and perfects me, is better than any gift I could have given him while he lived. It is a variation of our wedding vows to each other before God so many years ago. Those vows said " 'til death do us part," but I much prefer to believe that they endure for all eternity.

And it is this ultimate gift of shared unity that fills our empty hearts as Christmas approaches.

The gift freely given by God is eternal life in Christ Jesus our Lord. **Rom 6:23**

THIRD THURSDAY OF ADVENT

St Augustine wrote a beautiful letter (Letter 130) to a Roman widow who asked him to write to her on how to pray. One point he makes is that a widow is desolate (in Latin desolata) *which means "left alone" as well as "sorrowful"—-the two pretty much go together. He points out that everyone who really believes in God and is in touch with her deepest reality is essentially alone until she returns to the God who made and redeemed her. Monk also means "the solitary one," so the widow is a hidden monk!*

Letter from Abbot John Eudes Bamberger, OCSO

ONE THING THAT MAKES ME SAD is my unconscious use of the word "we," and the present tense. I often find myself saying "We've lived here for fifteen years," or "We like that restaurant," or "We always go to the 5 p.m. Mass." Sadly, all widows have to re-learn the single pronoun as well as the single life, but after many years of marriage, it requires time. It is a change that I have not come close to making, and my guess is that it will take years. It's not only grammatical usage but also a new way of thinking and of viewing one's existence. I need to learn to downsize myself from two into one. Particularly at Christmastime, the process is excruciating, because the season focuses on couples and families. That is why it is so difficult to be with other people during the Christmas season, particularly when they are surrounded by their own loved ones. Well-intentioned friends invite me to join them, but it only heightens my feelings of isolation and loneliness. How will I ever be able to fill this emptiness?

We feel like mere remnants of our former selves, diminished by our loss. Trying to fill this emptiness is perhaps the cruelest, most difficult challenge of the grieving process. It is surely the most painful. Some people simply can't bear it, and for a long time just go through their day as in a vacuum, unable to face anything ahead of them beyond the next fifteen minutes. Others try frantically to fill their emptiness with things to do, places to go, and people to see. Some may turn to alcohol, medication, or just stay in bed.

What can compensate for a loss as great as a missing limb? The analogy is apt. When someone loses a leg, an enormous part of him is permanently severed and can never be recovered. His body is incomplete and wounded forever. The awareness of loss is his first shocking thought upon awakening, every day for the rest of his life. Yet it is possible to walk again. He won't look the same, feel the same, or be the same. There will always be some discomfort or even pain. Nonetheless it will be possible to get from one place to another, even if in a diminished capacity. For the bereaved, learning to get back into life is enormously difficult, but the effort must be made. The work is tiring and discouraging, but it must be done. One is admonished to get back on a horse right after falling, before the fear sets in. So it is with our life, which God wants us to live, not to shrink from.

But the emptiness, that enormous, strangling, panicky sense of being all alone, is unavoidable. As the Abbot wrote, the widow is desolate. And at no time is the awareness greater than at this season of the year, as the solitary heart gapes like an empty Christmas stocking.

I'll have a blue Christmas without you
I'll be so blue thinking about you
Decorations of red
On a green Christmas tree
Won't be the same
If you're not here with me

From "Blue Christmas," J. Johnson, B. Hayes

THIRD FRIDAY OF ADVENT

Nature abhors a vacuum.   **Francois Rabelais, 1553**

WE FEEL ISOLATED AND NUMB, yet struggling for gratitude; sad, yet yearning for Christmas joy; empty-hearted, yet wanting to give of ourselves to both the Infant Jesus and to our missing loved one. How do we make something meaningful out of such contradictions? My heart these days feels like a cold, unmoving stone. But hearts that don't move can die. God has not chosen to call me to him at this time, so I must jump-start my heart for him and live out the days that he has allotted to me. As for the emptiness in it, the aching void must be filled with something even more perfect than any human relationship. Nothing earthly could ever satisfy it again, not people or possessions, not travel or money. The answer, simply, is that the only solution for a broken heart is turning to God, and allowing him to fill it with his mercy and love and, in so doing, to heal it and draw it to him. I believe that with God's grace, this is possible.

According to an ancient Chinese proverb: *"The longest journey begins with the first step."* And so it is with anyone who has to rebuild, whether it is a house in the aftermath of a storm or one's life following the death of a loved one. The physical part is hard enough, in dealing with personal possessions, deciphering finances, and notifying friends. But an even more difficult project is rearranging the heart and soul in order to replenish their balance. The first step is and must always be *prayer*. At first that prayer will be like the prayer of a child, desperate, incredulous, anguished. It will go through and return to different stages over and over, as we move through denial and panic and that overwhelming feeling that we can't possibly make it by ourselves.

One recollection I have of being profoundly moved by prayer shortly after John's death was while reading Psalm 34 in the *Liturgy of the Hours* one Saturday morning, particularly the verse, *"The Lord is close to the broken hearted; those whose spirit is crushed He will save."* And about two weeks after the funeral I knelt in front of the tabernacle at church and whispered aloud, "Oh Jesus, I am so alone now." At once I sensed the reply, "You are never alone; I am with you always."

As time goes on, if we are faithful to the Lord in prayer, he will manifest himself to us in small assurances of comfort. They will be very slight manifestations, like that still, small voice heard by Elijah. But if we allow ourselves the meditative silence in which to hear him, we will. This is different from empty silence, in which we are only aware of the one who is missing, the absence of their voice and their laugh. Meditative silence is both prayerful and creative, and means listening for the Lord and speaking to him in our hearts. It may be several months before there is sufficient calm within us to learn how to listen, but we must not give up. God is all we have and all there is during our sorrow, because he is eternally present and is with us in a way we cannot fathom. In time, we move from overwhelming loss to the gradual realization that he will never leave us.

I will come to you in the silence
I will lift you from all your fear
You will hear My voice
I claim you as My choice
Be still, and know I am near

I am hope for all who are hopeless
I am eyes for all who long to see
In the shadows of the night,
I will be your light
Come and rest in Me

"You Are Mine," David Haas, 1991

THIRD SATURDAY OF ADVENT

I sought the Lord and he answered me; he set me free from all my fears. In my anguish I cried out; the Lord heard my plea, and I was saved from all my troubles. The Lord remains close to the brokenhearted, and he saves those whose spirit is crushed.

Ps 34:5, 7, 19

THIS AWARENESS OF STRENGTH and protection from God will be our sustenance and will facilitate our ability to return to some measure of "normal" life, although our life will never be the way it was before our loss. It will be a new normal, one fashioned on the foundation of our grief but also of our resilience. The great German Lutheran theologian Dietrich Bonhoeffer wrote beautifully about this:

> Nothing can console us when we lose a beloved person and no one should try. We have to simply bear and survive it. That sounds hard but is in fact a great consolation: When the hole remains unfilled, we rèmain connected through it. It is wrong to say that God fills the gap, because he keeps it empty and so helps us to sustain our old communion, even through pain. The more beautiful and fulfilling our memories, the harder the separation. But gratefulness transforms the agony of memory into a quiet joy. We should avoid burrowing in our memories, just as we do not look at

a precious gift continuously. Rather, we should rather save them for special hours, like a hidden treasure of which we are certain. Then a pervading joy and strength will flow from the past.

As Bonhoeffer points out, we should never try to fill in the emptiness entirely, but the painful part can be closed, the part that is dead, stagnant space. As the new stirrings of hope begin, it is interesting to note that our sorrow doesn't diminish. Well-meaning friends continue to say "In time, it will get better." What really happens is that the pain moves over and allows a certain hope to move in as well, somewhat like an old fashioned balancing scale. The lucky person is the one in whom, after some time, the weights will be equal. As Christmas approaches, we can see that the foreknowledge of the Passion does not diminish the brightness of the Star. There is room in our hearts for both.

You, however, do not live according to the flesh but according to the Spirit, since the Spirit of God dwells in you.   **Rom 8:9**

Special Readings
December 17-24

Fourth Week of Advent

O Antiphons,

Winter Solstice

DECEMBER 17TH—O WISDOM

O Wisdom, that proceeds from the mouth of the Most High, reaching from end to end mightily, and sweetly disposing all things: come and teach us the way of prudence.

EVERY YEAR I LOOK FORWARD to the "O Antiphons" that are recited at Vespers of the *Liturgy of the Hours* beginning on December 17th. It's the same feeling one gets turning onto the wide Via della Conciliazione in Rome and seeing St. Peter's Basilica at the end of the avenue, sort of a deep-in-the-stomach, "There it is!" sensation. Only in this case, it's, "Here he is! Our Savior is about to be born." Shopping not finished, presents not wrapped, menus not planned? No matter; the Lord is near. Bereft, brokenhearted, lonely? No matter; he whom the heavens cannot contain will be born as a man to redeem us and take away our tears and sorrow.

The first of the seven prayers asks for Wisdom; how perfect for one who grieves! There is a tendency to confront God with our unspoken question: How could you let this happen? Then we remember God's reply when Job challenged him: *"Who is this that darkens counsel by words of ignorance. . . .Where were you when I laid the foundation of the earth? Tell me, if you have understanding"* (Job 38:2, 4). So after we rant and rave and ask the Lord, "Why?" we are chastened. We realize that in the end, we have no answers and we don't know, and never will, why it happened. Nor do we need to. As a toddler can't fathom his parents' withholding something he wants but that is not good for him, we will never understand why it is that, although God always answers our prayers, sometimes the answer is no, or not now. We may never stop trying to put God into a box. We think that God "should" do things because they seem right to us. We have such reasoned logic, such clarity of thought, so of course God should see things through our eyes and do as we ask!

When we are prostrate with grief, we recognize our limitation. Mother Angelica of EWTN wrote, *"It is humbling to reach a point which I cannot pass—a point where a created mind realizes its capacity is too small to encompass the Infinite."* God, although present to us in ways we cannot fathom, is beyond our capacity to analyze. He is Wisdom itself and is in a dimension far greater than life, death, or mere human understanding.

Trying to unlock the secrets of God's eternal wisdom is like trying to number the grains of sand on the shore. It won't work. Life and death are beyond our grasp, as is the mind of their Creator. It is perhaps enough to read what the sacred author of the Book of Wisdom had to say about those who have died: *"The souls of the righteous are in the hand of God, and no torment shall touch them. In the eyes of the foolish, they seemed to be dead; and their departure was thought to be a disaster, and their going from us, utter destruction; but they are at peace"* (Wis 3:1-4).

Oh, the depth of the riches and wisdom and knowledge of God! How inscrutable are his judgments and how unfathomable his ways! For who has known the mind of the Lord, or who has been his counselor?

Rom 11:33-34

DECEMBER 18TH—O ADONAI

O Adonai, and Leader of the House of Israel, who appeared unto Moses in the burning bush, and gave him the law on Sinai: come and redeem us by Thy outstretched arm.

I THINK OF *ADONAI* as an elemental Hebrew word, used repeatedly in Jewish prayers that began *"Baruch atah Adonai elohaynu,"* or "Praise to you, Adonai our God." It is a name bestowed upon God in the Old Testament and means Lord or Ruler. It resonates with more majesty than our English word, Lord. It says clearly that God is "the Lord, God, the mighty God, the great king over all the gods" (Psalm 95). That thought, and that title, make us aware of our littleness and insignificance before him. As we approach Christmas and Jesus' birth in Bethlehem, we see ourselves humbly approaching the manger, not with kingly gifts but with all of our insecurities, shortcomings and needs.

The grieving person's hands seem especially empty at Christmas time. We come before the newborn King brokenhearted, frustrated by the joy and music and fellowship of the season that we enjoyed for so many years. What can we, so bereft, possibly bring to the Lord of Lords? He has already stated what he wants: *"Offer to God a sacrifice of thanksgiving and fulfill your vows to the Most High. Then if you cry out to me in time of trouble, I will rescue you, and you will honor me"*(Ps 50:14-16). What he really desires is our love and our fidelity. In return, he will console our broken hearts and we will glorify him for all eternity. In time our anguish will turn to everlasting joy if we are faithful now. God, more than anyone, knows the depth of our misery. He is Adonai, the Lord, who made our hearts which are now so full of sorrow. Our grief, too, is precious to him because through it we share in his Passion. Perhaps he treasures sorrowful hearts in a special way, knowing how difficult it is for us to lift them to him. When we do, it is likely that he keeps them close to his own.

Hear my voice in supplication as I plead for your help, as I lift up my hands toward your Most Holy Place.

Ps 28:2

DECEMBER 19TH—O ROOT OF JESSE

O Root of Jesse, who stands as the ensign of the people, before whom kings shall not open their lips; to whom the Gentiles shall pray: come and deliver us, tarry now no more.

THIS IS A FAMILIAR ADVENT SYMBOL, mentioned in hymns and in Mass readings. Isaiah promises us *"A shoot shall come out from the stump of Jesse, and out of his roots a bud shall blossom"* (Isa 11:1). This refers to Christ's ancestor, Jesse, King David's father. You may see a "Jesse tree" in your church at Christmas bearing various Christian symbols showing that Jesus was the fruit or bloom from that lineal tree.

In central New Mexico, December is a bleak month in terms of climate. The mountains are brown , sometimes topped with snow, and the grass on the hillsides is yellowed and parched. Bitter winds sweep across the arroyos leaving them dry and barren, and the red clay soil becomes hardened with frost. But hiking in the foothills of the Sandia Mountains, I have seen some lovely things. Underneath rocks or bushes, there are occasional cactus flowers blooming or in full bud, even on very cold days. Underneath all that brown, desolate landscape there are signs of life and dormancy that couldn't wait to burst forth into new growth. Tiny green buds can be spotted right next to patches of snow or brittle tumbleweed. This is symbolic of Christ, the bud on the stem of Jesse, our hope and promise in the midst of death and aridity.

What great comfort this provides for the bereaved! It is a metaphor not only for our own life to be able to return to a semblance of normalcy and hope, but also to remind us that our loved one's life has been transformed into a thing of eternal beauty. Like the tiny yellow flower growing out of the barren ground, both our hearts and their souls are always in possession of the newness of life in Christ. He consoles our grieving spirits with his love and his nearness, as he promises that his burden is light, that we should not be afraid, that he will always be with us. Similarly, he gives our departed ones their eternal reward for a lifetime of fidelity to him on earth, and provides them with joy and peace incomprehensible to our finite minds. Our grief is for ourselves and for our loss; it would surely be wasted on those who have died, who now live in perpetual glory with Almighty God.

It is Christ, the fruition of his Father's everlasting glory, the "rose e'er blooming from tender stem hath sprung,"[3] who flowers in our hearts and souls at Christmas. May our hearts turn to him in wonder and love and hope for our own new beginning.

---

[3] "Lo, How a Rose E'er Blooming," 15th century carol

And again Isaiah asserts, "The root of Jesse shall come, the one who will arise to rule the Gentiles; the Gentiles will hope in him." May the God of hope fill you with all joy and peace in believing, so that you may grow rich in hope by the power of the Holy Spirit. **Rom 15:12**

DECEMBER 20TH—O KEY OF DAVID

O Key of David , O royal Power of Israel controlling at your will the gate of heaven: come, break down the prison walls of death for those who dwell in darkness and the shadow of death; and lead your captive people into freedom.

KEYS ARE USED FOR GETTING IN and going out, for entering and securing. They are a means to entry, and also a way to shut things out for protection. When we misplace our keys we feel powerless. When we experience the death of a spouse, we feel that not only have we lost our key to happiness, but also the key to life itself. We cannot recover the existence that we enjoyed as a couple, and we can't imagine ever regaining any sense of normalcy. Our sorrow can easily turn into panic that washes over us in huge waves, like nausea. These anxiety attacks can cause an amazing variety of physical symptoms like shortness of breath, loss of appetite, insomnia, and a pounding heart. How curious that a pain which begins in the mind can spread so quickly throughout our body. In my own case, I don't think that it will ever fully go away, and it comes up often and unexpectedly as memories are triggered on a daily basis. It feels as though those nerve endings will always be raw. If we have seemingly lost the key to the life we knew, we must find a way to unlock the door to a meaningful daily existence. We need to remember that the one we grieve for would have wanted that, and, in fact, demanded our efforts to do so.

If the first step in this journey is *prayer,* the second one has to be *hope.* The newly bereaved can't help being irritated by the sprightly smiles of people who promise us "it will get better." In many ways it won't, but we will learn new ways. We will learn to navigate our way again, one hesitant step at a time. It will be painful, but we will do it. If that seems grim, there is hope: we are never alone in our new, hesitant way of learning to live again without the one we love. There really is a key which will unlock the seemingly impassable barrier to our progress, and perhaps even our joy. That key is Christ. At the Last Supper, the apostle Thomas said to him, *"Lord, we do not know where you are going. How can we know the way?"* Jesus' reply was not for Thomas alone when he answered, *"I am the way, and the truth, and the life. No one comes to the Father except through me"*(Jn 14:5, 6). Jesus himself will be the key that unlocks the door for us as well. The challenge we face is to follow—step by painful step. Some days, especially in the very beginning, progress is impossible, the heartache indescribable. Even months or years later, a simple thought, song or memory can reopen the floodgates. This is when Christ is closest to us, as we try to unite our pain to his in Gethsemane, to Mary's at Golgotha, and to that of our brothers and sisters who suffer throughout the world.

Five months after John died, our pastor preached on suffering, saying: "Anything we offer to the Lord, he will use." This made me think of a spiritual gift card with which we can donate consolation. On a particularly bad day when I was so overwhelmed with grief that I felt as though I would split apart, I cried out to God to take my pain and to apply it to the person in the world most in need of his comfort at that moment—a parent whose child had just been removed from life support, a military wife who had just been told of her husband's death in combat, an addicted drunk lying abandoned in a city gutter. Doing this transforms our pain and makes it useful, turns it from an ugly, repugnant thing into an implement of hope. We can't do it alone; God has to be the one who transforms it. Being able to do this is our special key to a new beginning, our way of looking forward, which will help us to get back some of the balance that was lost in our lives.

Do not be grieved, for the joy of the Lord is your strength.
Neh 8:10

DECEMBER 21ST—THE WINTER SOLSTICE

O Radiant Dawn, splendor of eternal light, sun of justice: come, shine on those who dwell in darkness and the shadow of death.

ONE OF THE MOST PROFOUND PAIRINGS, of Christmas hope and sorrow from grief, occurs in this beautiful antiphon. Today is the longest night of the year and consequently has the shortest amount of daylight. It is a good metaphor for those who grieve, for whom the hours of darkness seem to far outnumber those of light. We find ourselves in a night without end, an existence without a future. The sun seems to have set on our happiness and we feel that the darkness will overwhelm us.

Yet dawn comes. Even when we don't see it or don't care, the sky brightens and the sun rises. The day goes on and so does life. It is up to us whether to be observers or participants. We may not feel up to participating yet, and it might require great effort to be interested. When John first died, I couldn't read the paper or watch the news. I was too restless, too agitated, simply too caught up in my own anguish. I didn't care about the world or anyone in it but myself and my own pain. Although normal and understandable for a while, ultimately this mindset is destructive. God created the earth and all of its creatures for our use and pleasure. Then he created us out of his great love, telling us, *"Do not fear, for I have redeemed you; I have called you by name: you are mine"*(Isa 43:1). Finally, he sent his Son to save us, to die for our sins and to open heaven to us for our eternal joy.

Who are we, in the face of such magnanimity, to pout and decide that we no longer care? This is defiance as well as ingratitude. It doesn't mean that we will dance and sing and laugh easily. Some days it takes great effort to manage even a smile. But underneath all the sorrow there must be gratitude, for all life is a gift from God. Just because we aren't feeling it doesn't make it any less true.

At the end of our life we will see everlasting day, which will be brightened simply by God's presence all around us. Our loved one is enjoying that right now. We are literally still in darkness, but some day, *"because of the tender mercy of our God . . . the dawn from on high will break upon us to shine on those who sit in darkness and in the shadow of death, to guide our feet along the path of peace"* (Lk 1:78-79). We can take the symbolism of the Winter Solstice and make it a metaphor for the cold, dark sorrow of the world which ends with the dawn of God's radiant love, filling our souls with hope and gladness.

You would do well to pay close attention to (the voice of God), as to a lamp shining in a dark place, until day dawns and the morning star rises in your hearts.

2 Pet 1:19

DECEMBER 22ND—O KING OF ALL NATIONS

O King of all nations, the only joy of every human heart;
O Keystone of the mighty arch of man, come and save the
creature you fashioned from the dust.

THIS ANTIPHON ADDRESSES the profundity of the Incarnation. Jesus is not only a sweet infant on a greeting card, he is also Almighty God, who in the act of the most incredible loving condescension, far beyond our ability to imagine, took upon himself our humble human flesh and lived as a man, dying in the ignominy of the Cross. Just as it would have seemed more appropriate for him to have been born into wealth, lying on a silk coverlet, we also feel that he should have died a natural death as an old man, surrounded by skilled doctors and loving friends. Instead, as a young man, he was nailed to rough wood and hung dying in the hot sun, dripping with blood and sweat. *"Hail, King of the Jews!"* scoffed the Roman soldiers contemptuously (Mt 15:18). What does Christ's passion and death have to do with Christmas? Everything! Christmas is all about his humanity. It is the story of love, of a God who so loved us—the pinnacle of his creation— that he was born of a woman to become part of us; who so loved us in spite of our sinful nature that he died for us. And this human child is our King. He is the *summum bonum,* the supreme good and ultimate power, almighty God himself. At this season we sing Isaiah's words set to Handel's music: *"His name will be called Wonderful*

Counselor, Mighty God, Everlasting Father, Prince of Peace"(Isa 9:6).

A nineteenth century American folk hymn asks:

What wondrous love is this, O my soul, O my soul!
What wondrous love is this, O my soul!
What wondrous love is this
that caused the Lord of bliss
to lay aside his crown for my soul,
to lay aside his crown for my soul?[4]

Thus, the giver of all gifts has become our Gift. That is the story of Christmas in its deepest essence. It is the reason why, even if our hearts are breaking, we must pause to raise our eyes in awe and wonder at the miracle that we celebrate anew each year. As we receive him on Christmas in Holy Communion, that gift is intensified because it becomes tangible. He gives us himself in the flesh, a gift wrapped not in ribbon but in grace, a gift that will never lose its luster but grow brighter in our souls. Who are we that we should be the recipients of such a Gift? No one at all except God's chosen children, whom he loves with "an everlasting love"(Isa 31:3).

Thanks be to God for his indescribable gift! **2 Cor 9:15**

---

[4] "Wondrous Love," from *The Southern Harmony,* 1835

DECEMBER 23RD—O EMMANUEL

O Emmanuel, king and lawgiver, desire of the nations, Savior of all people: come and set us free, lord our God.

THE TIME OF ADVENT is nearly over and Christmas is very close. People in the grocery store ask, "Are you all ready for Christmas?" Of course not! The presents may be wrapped, the mistletoe hung and the turkey thawing, but in our hearts, how can plans ever be complete to receive the Son of God? Happily, it is a lifetime project of preparation, of continually cleansing our souls through the sacrament of Penance, softening our souls through the practice of virtue, and purifying our souls in the frequent reception of the Eucharist.

Our grief is raw, perhaps more so as we witness the world's attempt at seasonal joy. The contrast is poignant when we see couples holding hands or purchasing special presents for other family members. Here is where we must remember that we, too, have had our time of gifts, and of a love that, in the end, will last forever. This is not the time for self-reflection of a morose kind. It is time to look inward only as we present ourselves to the Christ Child and as we accept him as the everlasting gift in return. For unlike the other trappings of Christmas that get packed away in the attic in January, Our Lord stays. The word Emmanuel means "God with us" (Mt 1:23). He is here, not for a day or even a season, but for eternity. As long as we are in the state of grace, as long as we struggle to remain true to him because he is our God who so loved us as to be born as a tiny child, he will be with us. At the end of the Eucharistic Prayer of the Mass, the priest prays the doxology: "Through him, with him, and in him." No one who grieves, regardless of feelings of fear and bewilderment, no matter how empty and silent their home, is ever truly alone. For in the center of their being their savior rests, as surely as he lay in the manger in Bethlehem. He is our Lord, our God with us, for as long as we can offer him a home within ourselves. He is not just a guest but rather becomes the host, welcoming us into himself as he dwells within us. It is a beautiful mystery to contemplate; it is a beautiful thing to experience.

Christ be with me, Christ within me,
Christ behind me, Christ before me,
Christ beside me, Christ to win me,
Christ to comfort and restore me,
Christ beneath me, Christ above me,
Christ in quiet, Christ in danger,
Christ in hearts of all that love me,
Christ in mouth of friend and stranger.

St. Patrick

DECEMBER 24TH-25TH—CHRISTMAS: SON SHINE

Almighty God and Father of light, a child is born for us and a son is given to us. Your eternal word leaped down from heaven in the silent watches of the night, and now your Church is filled with wonder at the nearness of her God. Open our hearts to receive His life and increase our vision with the rising of dawn, that our lives may be filled with His glory and His peace, who reigns for ever and ever.

Liturgy of the Hours, **Morning Prayer for Christmas**

LORD, I AM AWAKE but my eyes aren't open yet. Even so, this day feels different. It is a special day, the anniversary of the day that changed the world. Part of me wants to stay in bed, yet I smile in remembrance of the lines from *A Christmas Carol,* when Ebenezer Scrooge leaps from his bed, asks a boy in the street what day it is, and then says, "It's Christmas Day! I haven't missed it!" I will burrow in my bed for a moment, Lord, to think about that. I haven't missed it. John is not here and everything has changed. And yet, it's Christmas, the feast of the Incarnation. And God has said, "Behold, I am making all things new" (Rev 21:5). Does John celebrate Christmas with you in heaven today, Lord? Do he and all the holy people who have died, other spouses, parents, children, friends—do they somehow kneel before the Christ Child and see him as he was that day in Bethlehem? What is it like to see you face to face?

I won't see you in person today, Jesus, but I will receive you in the Eucharist. I will see you in the faces of friends and family later in the day. I will see how, even in this troubled world, the spirit of your birth has touched much of mankind, for one day at least, with joy and peace and happiness.

I won't see John in person today either, and that breaks my heart. He was such a blessing. Thank you, Lord, for the precious gift of his life and companionship and love for all those years. If you see him in the company of your saints today, Lord, tell him that. And bless all of those poor souls who awaken today without those happy memories, who are widowed, divorced, or in troubled marriages, or who grieve for a child, parent or friend.

As this year winds to a close, Lord, I look back on it with astonishment that I made it this far! I have been so sad and so lost for a large portion of it, scarcely noticing as the months went by. I couldn't have made it without you there to hold me up, to guide me and give me strength and grace to go on with life. I thought in many ways that my life was over, but I know that I was wrong. Each remaining hour, day and year that is left to me is your gift, and your challenge to follow in your footsteps. Someday you will welcome me into your kingdom as you did John, and you will both be there waiting for me.

I must get up now, Lord. Today is a new beginning. There are gifts to be exchanged. There is my lifelong gratitude for the precious gift of my husband. And most of all, this day marks the coming of the greatest gift of all time, the Son of God, to save all people from the darkness of sin and to direct them toward the light of their eternal destiny.

This day is holy to the Lord your God. Do not mourn or weep . . . for this day is holy to the Lord and do not be grieved, for the joy of the Lord is your strength!

Neh 8:9, 10

PRAYER RESOURCES

LESSONS FOR LIVING
FROM THE 23RD PSALM
Victor M. Parachin

". . . serves us great morsels of faith from wise brothers and sisters of ages past and present whose individual stories . . . prove again how sewn together we all are in our humanness, and how, especially in the hard-to-understand destructive days of life, Divine love never leaves us. "
—Antoinette Bosco

RP 130/04 ISBN 978-1-878718-91-4   **$6.95**

HOW SHALL WE PRAY?
30 Steps to Prayer
James F. Gaffney

"Presents a tempting feast of prayer styles, sure to satisfy the cravings of readers seeking to deepen their grasp of what prayer means in the context of day-to-day living."   **—Lorraine Murray**

RP 136/04 ISBN 978-1-878718-94-5   **$5.95**

PRAYING THE LORD'S PRAYER
WITH MARY
An Imaginative Meditation
Susan Muto and Adrian van Kaam

". . . wipes away our preconceived notions and reveals the truly revolutionary nature of the Lord's prayer."
—Catholic Library World

RP 150/04   ISBN 978-1-878718-67-9   **$8.95**

YOU ARE MY BELOVED
Meditations on God's Steadfast Love
Mitch Finley

"Mitch Finley strips away all our fears, defenses, and foolishness to point out the joy and opportunity in acknowledging and gracefully accepting God's limitless love for us."   **—Ron Hansen**

RP 115/04 ISBN 978-1-878718-49-5   **$10.95**

www.catholicbookpublishing.com

ADDITIONAL RESOURCES

A PARTY OF ONE
Meditations for Those Who Live Alone

"Would be as useful for the widow or widower as it would be for the college student or young person beginning a first job."

—*Crux of the News*

No. RP 744/04 ISBN 978-1-933066-01-1   **$5.95**

THE SPIRITUAL SPA
Getting Away without Going Away

Specially designed tasks—undertaken independently or with a favorite few—teach us how to spiritually relax, interiorly surrender and step into the refreshing pool of God's grace.

No. RP 745/04   **$9.95**
ISBN 978-1-878718-99-0

OUR GROUNDS FOR HOPE

"This book will console sufferers who seek and see hope in the cross of Jesus Christ."

—*Susan Muto, Ph.D.*

No. RP 124/04   **$1.95**
ISBN 978-1-878718-56-3

BOOKS BY ADOLFO QUEZADA

SABBATH MOMENTS

A six-week prayer format using Scripture, reflection and prayer to soothe your mind, body and soul.

No. RP 178/04   **$6.95**
ISBN 978-1-878718-80-8

LOVING YOURSELF FOR GOD'S SAKE

. . . gently directs the reader to see the gift of self in an entirely new and beautiful light.

No. RP 720/04   **$5.95**
ISBN 978-1-878718-35-8

HEART PEACE

". . . one of the most authentic books . . . on the gut-wrenching conditions that cause or lead to human suffering."

—*Antoinette Bosco*

No. RP 117/04   **$9.95**
ISBN 978-1-878718-52-5

www.catholicbookpublishing.com

Additional Titles Published by Resurrection Press, a Catholic Book Publishing Imprint

For a free catalog call 1-800-892-6657
www.catholicbookpublishing.com